HOW TO WRITE

STORIES

CELIA WARREN

QED Publishing

First published in the UK in 2007 by
QED Publishing
A Quarto Group company
226 City Road
London EC1V 2TT
www.qed-publishing.co.uk

A Catalogue record for this book is available from the British Library.

ISBN 978 1 84835 203 2

Written by Celia Warren
Designed by Jackie Palmer
Editor Louisa Somerville
Illustrations by Tim Loughead
Consultant Anne Faundez

Publisher Steve Evans
Creative Director Zeta Davies
Senior Editior Hannah Ray

Printed and bound in China

Words in **bold** are explained in the glossary on page 30.

CONTENTS

STORY GENRES

Anyone who makes up stories and writes them down is an **author**. You can be an author, too! The wonderful thing about being an author is that you can be anyone, go anywhere, do anything you like. If you want to sprout wings and fly or be a deep-sea diver, you can! You can do anything in your imagination. If you turn it into a story, then others can share your adventures in **fiction**. Take a look at some of the **genres** of story – but don't forget, some books can fit into more than one genre.

Did you know?

The name Wendy did not exist until the author J.M. Barrie wrote Peter Pan just over 100 years ago. He invented the name after he heard a young child say "my wendy", meaning "my friendy" (my friend).

- **Fairy stories, legends and folk tales**
  Well-known traditional tales – including *Goldilocks and the Three Bears* and *The Frog Prince* – and **legends** such as those featuring Robin Hood and Odysseus.

- **Fables and parables**
  Stories with a moral or a message, including such Bible stories as *The Prodigal Son* and *The Good Shepherd*, and Aesop's **fables**, such as *The Hare and the Tortoise*.

- **Historical**
  Stories set in the past, such as *Goodnight Mr Tom* by Michelle Magorian. They can be about real or fictional events.

Some authors' fictional **characters** are so convincing that they become as much a part of life as if they were real people. You'd know Winnie the Pooh, Alice in Wonderland or Harry Potter if you met them in the street, wouldn't you?

- **Sci-fi (short for science fiction)**
  Stories inspired by scientific developments. They are usually set in the future and often involve aliens. The *Artemis Fowl* books by Eoin Colfer are sci-fi stories.

- **Fantasy**
  Stories whose characters or events are not based in reality. The reader must accept the writer's **fantasy** world. *The Lion, the Witch and the Wardrobe* by C.S. Lewis is a fantasy story.

- **Adventure and mystery**
  Stories about exciting and mystifying events, where readers try to solve the mystery along with the characters. *The Scarecrow and his Servant* by Philip Pullman is an adventure story.

Tips

- It's often best to write the sort of story that you would enjoy reading yourself.
- Read as many books in different genres as you can. The more you read, the more your own writing will improve.

- **Graphic stories**
  Stories, such as those about the adventures of Tintin or Asterix, told in pictures with words in speech bubbles and captions.

GATHERING IDEAS

Ideas for stories are everywhere. Something you see, hear or dream may spark off the inspiration for a story or, at least, an incident or a character. It's not always convenient to sit down and write straight away, so make notes when ideas occur to you.

Ideas notebook

Keep a notebook beside your bed or in your pocket – with a pen, of course. Jot down anything that pops into your head, even just a word. It could come in handy when creating a character or situation for a new story. You could write down:

- an overheard snippet of conversation (but don't eavesdrop!)
- bits of dreams – as soon as you wake up.
- something funny, unusual or interesting you see while walking in the park, such as a parent training a dog to find her children, a kite getting stuck in a tree or a child's ice cream toppling on to a toddler's head.
- a series of words that pop into your head from nowhere. For example:

"Floppy poppy!
Well, blow me down!"

Tip

When you're next in the mood for writing, open your notebook and see what you scribbled down – the seeds of ideas for stories. Now you can 'water' the seeds and watch them grow!

In the news

Newspapers are a great source of story ideas. Most news stories involve people (who can become your story's characters). For example, a new planet is discovered. Who are the scientists involved? What are they like? If the newspaper doesn't tell you, invent their characters for yourself.

Copycat?

Rewriting a newspaper story does not make it your own. The writer has the **copyright** of their article. You don't have the right to copy what they have written but you can take a real-life piece of news and draw information from it for a different story. So you could turn the discovery of a dinosaur into a story about an archaeologist who digs up a dinosaur skeleton that comes to life after everyone at the museum has gone home. This turns **facts** into fiction.

Springboard

Take a few words from a newspaper story or headline and use them as a story title. You are only using the words for the title, so your story will be nothing like the one in the newspaper. Here are some made-up headlines to start you off:

- Prince pays the price
- Polly the parrot keeps mum
- Cheesy does it!
- Smallest mammal discovered
- Rover to the rescue!

Tip

All stories involve a character – either human or animal – who has a problem that must be solved. Before you start writing, ask yourself: who is my story's main character and what is his or her problem?

Tip

Change the characters' names from those in real life – to something memorable, if possible. Professor Trudie Spligwort is quite a catchy name!

FROM FACT TO FICTION

It can be hard to get started with story writing. People often say, "Write about what you know". Writing from your own experience gives you confidence, but you can also describe what happens to others. Because your brain gathers knowledge from the world around you all the time, you don't need to have broken a bone yourself to have a character break a leg!

'I know...' plus 'what if...?'

Here's a way to write a story that moves from what you know to what you can only imagine. Using a pencil, write an account of something that has happened in your life, as if you were telling a friend or writing a diary. Read it through, with a pen handy. Ask yourself "What if ...?" and use the pen to change some things slightly and others dramatically, turning facts into fiction. Maybe you could introduce a fantasy element. Here's an example:

This morning, when I opened the curtains
the sky was green. My mouth fell open.
~~it was pouring with rain. I was annoyed as~~
M had planned a
~~m~~y friend Danny and I ~~were planning a~~ picnic by
the river. ~~Instead we decided to go to the cinema.~~
but the voice that answered
I rang Danny ~~and we arranged to meet at the bus-~~
sounded nothing like him.
~~stop and get the twelve-thirty bus into town.~~

***Edit** the **text** so that the **narrative** flows more smoothly.*

Check that your new words make sense alongside the original words that you're keeping.

Tip

In your writing, it is better to show than to tell. For example, 'I was annoyed' tells the reader how the author felt, but 'My mouth fell open' is much more expressive. It shows that the author was astounded without actually saying it.

Copy the start of your new story onto a fresh sheet of paper, like this:

Springboard

Write a story that begins and ends with the same phrase, such as:

- I never did like carrots.
- It was the first and last day I ever met my cousin.
- Dogs understand more than we think.

This morning, when I opened the curtains, the sky was green. My mouth fell open. My friend Danny and I had planned a picnic by the river. I rang Danny but the voice that answered sounded nothing like him.

The story now has lots of possibilities. Danny sounds different.

- Will he look different, too?
- Has Danny turned into someone else?
- Is the sky really green and, if so, why? Or are the writer's senses confused?

Ask yourself some 'what', 'where', 'why' and 'who' questions about your own story. Jot down ideas, so that you know roughly where the story is going and how it will end. Then write the rest of the story before your enthusiasm dwindles.

Springboard

- Imagine yourself shrinking or growing so that a familiar environment becomes threatening or dangerous.
- Have a fantasy character living your life. For example: what happens when a snowman eats porridge or sits next to the radiator at school?

BUILDING A STORY

Writing a story is a bit like building a house. You gather your materials – your words – but before you begin building you need a design. Here are the things you need for your story design:

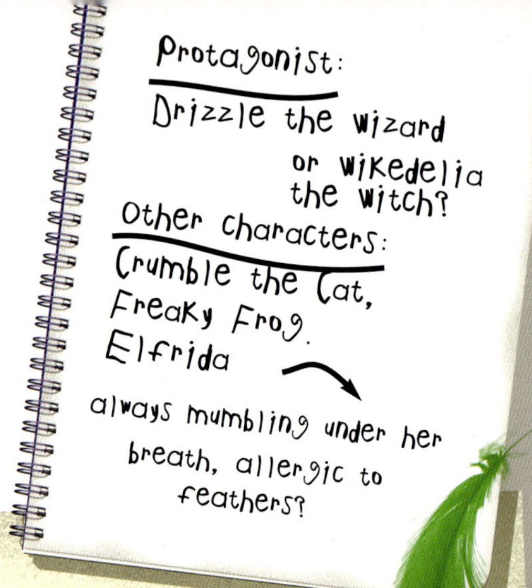

Setting

The setting is the time and place. It could be another planet in the future, a school or a pharaoh's palace. You may find it helps to imagine the setting as a theatre. Picture a stage for your character-actors with several backdrops for different scenes.

TIME: 3000 BCE
PLACE: Egypt
SCENES: The throne room of the Pharaoh's palace; a holy temple; the dark, winding corridors of a pyramid; a barge on the Nile.

Theme

The theme is the story's message. It may be something that the reader thinks about after they have read the story. For example, the theme may be 'you can overcome fear' or 'bad people don't win'.

Characters

The main character is called the **protagonist**. Try to make your readers care about this person and identify with them, which means being able to understand and share the character's thoughts and feelings. You can create characters that oppose the protagonist, or who influence events. (Use contrasting names to avoid your readers getting confused.) Use **dialogue** to show their personalities. Picture them: how do they speak? what habits do they have?

Don't create too many characters for you to remember!

Plot

What happens in which order and why, and with what outcome is called a **plot**. Making a timeline helps you to work out the plot. Mark the story's main events along the timeline.

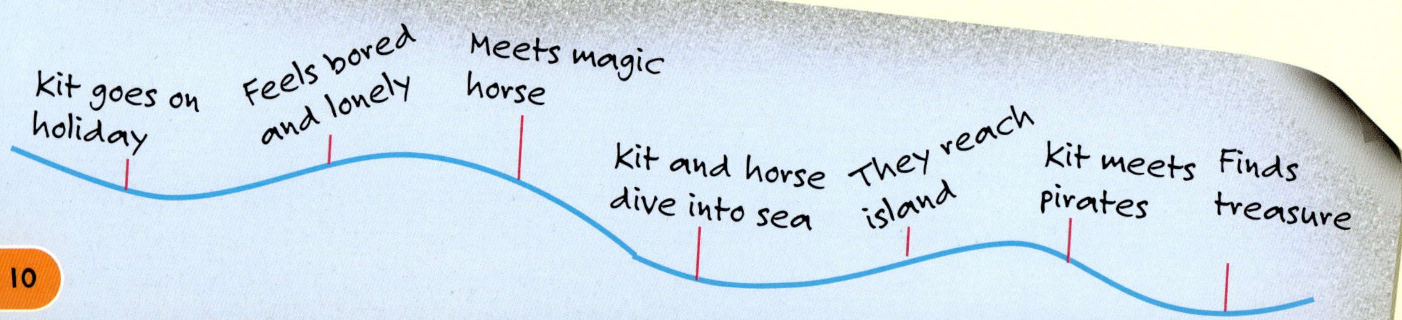

From start... to finish

Once you have your story's setting, characters and plot, it's time to start 'building'! Your story will have three parts: a beginning, a middle and an end.

Beginning

Make the start of your story short. Involve the reader straight away without too much description or detail. A good attention-grabber is to start with **direct speech**.

"Hey – that's my bike you're riding," shouted Jack.
The girl wobbled for a second as she glanced over her shoulder.
"Well, it's mine now," she said.

We learn several things:
The main character is called Jack.
There's a confrontation and problem to overcome.
Jack doesn't know the girl. (The author hasn't used her name – yet!)

Middle

Next, the characters develop and things happen in a string of connected events. The characters' actions influence events, which may, in turn, change the characters' feelings, attitudes or even their whole lives!

End

It is important to tie up all 'loose ends'. Don't leave your reader thinking, "But what about such-and-such?" Provide a satisfying outcome. It must leave the protagonist (and readers who care about him or her) feeling better off than at the start and with most – if not all – problems solved. We should be able to close the book content that we know what happened to all the characters.

Tip

A page of text could cover anything from a minute to half a lifetime, depending on the story length. Make the plot unfold fast enough to keep your readers' attention but slow enough for them to get to know the characters and share the action.

Springboard

Try building a story from these materials:

THEME: Lost SETTING: Fairground
PROTAGONIST: Young boy or girl
PLOT: Boy/girl has run away because they're unhappy. By the end of the story, the child is back home and the reader knows why the child was unhappy, how he or she was found and why the child is happier than he or she was before.

CREATING CHARACTERS

Creating a character is like making a new friend!

Believable characters are vital to a good story. They should seem like real people, so remember that nobody is all good or all bad. Even the nastiest character might be kind to dogs or love their mum! Even the nicest character has a weak spot – a streak of jealousy maybe. You decide – but beware! As your characters become more real, it can be hard to make them stay in the plot.

Character file

Keep a fact-file about each key character. The more you include, the more you will get to know them. Include their colouring, age, height and build, hobbies, pets, favourite food, sports team or anything else of interest. You could also note their greatest disappointment or ambition. Once their personalities are established, the characters will seem real in your story.

GRANDPA GREGOR'S CHARACTER FILE:

70 years old and frail; very straight, white hair; rimless specs; usually bent over but straightens up when speaking; listens to brass band music on his MP3 player; would like to have played the trombone.

Tip

Some friends may take offence at appearing in your stories, so if you base a character on someone you know, make sure to disguise them. If it's a boy, make him a girl, and so on. Change other details, such as their age, hair colour or height.

Showing emotion

People's facial expressions and body language reveal what they are feeling. Imagine your character. Then show rather than tell (see page 8) your reader about the character's feelings through their actions, reactions, dialogue and body language.

TELL: Raj was unhappy.
SHOW: Raj strolled slowly, his head down and shoulders hunched. He frowned hard and bit his lip.

Note: When showing, the adjective 'unhappy' doesn't appear. Nor does the verb 'cry' but we know Raj was close to tears!

ACTIVITY

Describe your own bedroom. Include details that inform the reader about you: your age, gender, interests, family and friends.

What's in a name?

Authors often pick names that reflect a character's looks or personality, such as Mr Happy, Penny Sweet or Old Mrs Longtooth. Choose unusual names to make it easier for you – and your readers – to remember who's who. For example, Jeannie Blacklake is more memorable than Jane Black.

Environment

Sometimes we learn about a character from their environment:

'The bedroom was untidy but, nevertheless, had an orderliness about it. A pile of pony books on the floor beside the unmade bed were sorted by size. A caged hamster shared a bookshelf with a cuddly toy rabbit that had obviously been well squeezed for most of its owner's ten years. Shoved to the back of a small desk lay a half-written letter. The depth of dust it lay under suggested it was unlikely ever to see the inside of an envelope.'

Tip

Use an online search-engine to find more ideas for names. Some authors choose names because of their meanings. For example 'Peter' means steadfast, strong and dependable. This website lists names and their meanings: www.behindthename.com

ACTIVITY

Describe Raj doing different things in different moods. Choose an activity and an emotion from each list.

Activity:	Emotion:
Playing with friends	Excited
Eating dinner	Bored
Climbing a steep hill	Impatient
Water-skiing	Lonely
Walking around the shops	Afraid

Springboard

Write a story that shows how a person changes because of what happens to them, such as overcoming a fear. Choose a name that suits the character and situation, such as Sally Fairweather or Daniel Strong.

MINDMAPPING

Each of the world's six billion people has at least one story to tell. If you add to that six billion imaginations, that makes limitless ideas! Here are some ways of coming up with plots and planning how they will develop:

Mindmapping

Take a single word, and write down absolutely anything relating to it. Give yourself just five minutes and *don't think too hard*!

Start with one of these words:
PAPER WALLS SPACE WATER

Choose one thought that you've come up with and do a further **mindmap** around that.

Now, think of an incident that involves one of your ideas. This incident can form part of a story or you can develop the whole plot around it.

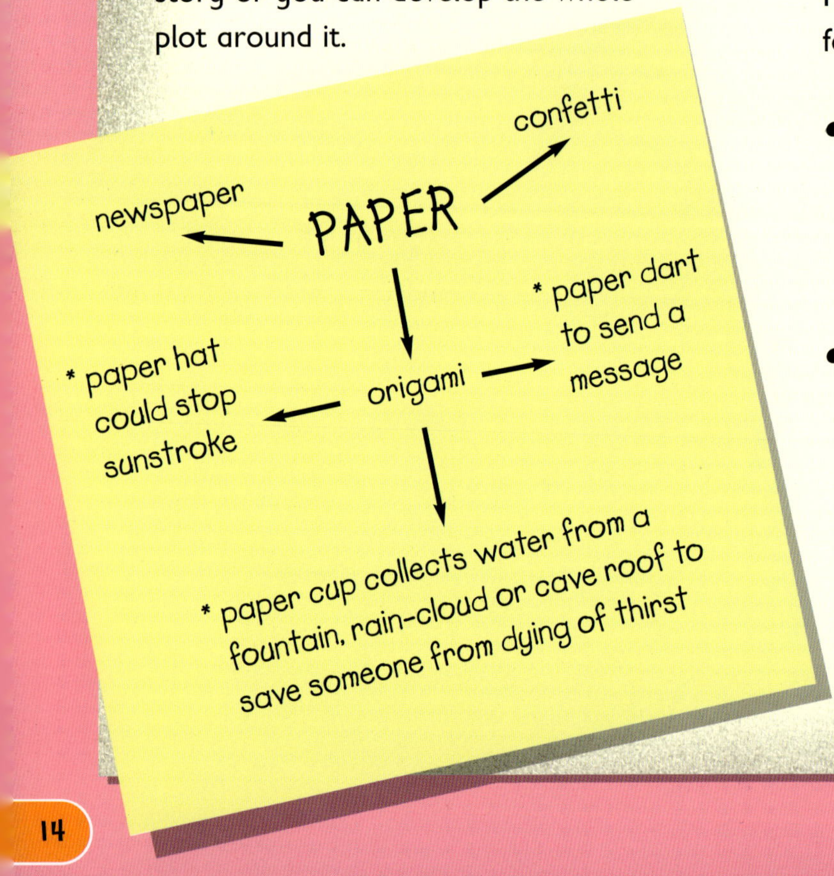

Good planning

Creating problems and solving each in turn makes for a good plot. As you plan your plot you will see how, as in real life, there isn't always one 'right' thing to do. Your characters will reach crossroads and have to choose a direction. Add a Happy Ending – even if there are tears on the way – or your readers will never forgive you!

What's the plot?

Plots usually involve one or both of the following:

- Thwarted ambition: someone or something stops the hero from getting what they want. They want to get from A to B but there are obstacles in the way.
- An emotional issue: a problem that involves a person's feelings and affects their lives. The hero goes on a 'personal journey' throughout the story. (This might also involve an actual journey to another place, such as a new home.)

Storyboarding

One helpful way to plan the plot is by **storyboarding**. Draw a series of boxes: one for each **paragraph**, if it's a short story; one for each **chapter** if it's a **novel**. In each box sketch the main event, as if it was an episode from a film. Use these pictures as a prompt for your writing. Or, write notes to remind you what will happen at each stage of the story. For example, here is a storyboard plan for *Little Red Riding Hood:*

Springboard

Make a storyboard for your favourite story or fairy tale. You don't need to use full sentences, just briefly jot down – or sketch – the main events in order.

Little Red Riding Hood

Mother tells Little Red Riding Hood to put on cloak and take cake to Grandma who is ill in bed on other side of forest.	LRRH in wood, stops to picks flowers on way, not noticing a wolf spying on her.	Wolf asks where she is going. She tells him where and why, and he bids farewell and disappears.
LRRH arrives at G'ma's and finds her looking odd: eyes too big, ears too big ; wolf fobs her off ("All the better to see / hear you with"). LRRH mentions G'ma's huge teeth.	G'ma says "All the better to eat you with" – leaps from bed to attack LRRH who sees wolf is dressed up in G'ma's nightie.	LRRH screams and her dad (who is a woodman felling trees nearby) arrives with axe and kills wolf. They find G'ma shut in wardrobe.

DECISIONS, DECISIONS

Before you start writing you must decide about viewpoint (whether you, yourself, are in the story – or not) and **tense** (whether you will be writing in the past or present tense).

Point of view

From whose viewpoint are you writing?

- You can be an observer, rather as if you were watching a film. If so, you will write in the 'third person': *he, she, they, his, her, their* are useful pronouns.
- You can write as one of the characters, as if you were inside the story. If so, you will be writing in the 'first person': *I, me, my; we, us, our* are useful pronouns.

Past or present?

Are you telling the story in the past or present tense?

- The past tense is the most usual and perhaps the easiest way of story telling: *He went…they chose…it was fun…*
- The present tense is less usual but can be useful – especially as a contrast, for a character relating an event or a dream: *I am…I choose…It is fun…*

ACTIVITY

Read the opening lines of some stories you have enjoyed. What have the authors said, and how have they said it? Which viewpoint have they taken? Did they write in the past or present tense? Plan an opening sentence, or paragraph, that will grab your readers by the throat. Rewrite it, changing the viewpoint and tense. How does it affect your writing's impact?

Tip

Even if you are writing fantasy, it must be believable to your readers. Make up the 'rules' for your fantasy world – and stick to them. If your character suddenly sprouts wings to escape from a lion, that's too easy a way out. On the other hand, the character could ride on the back of a winged creature to escape.

Symbols

Before you begin to write, you must also decide if you will use **symbols** in your story. Symbols are things that stand for something. Colours are often used as symbols. For example, the colour red may symbolize danger. In the story of *Little Red Riding Hood,* her red cloak warns the reader of trouble ahead. Symbols are not always colours. For example, a dove is a symbol of peace and love, like the dove in the Bible story of *Noah's Ark*.

Animal symbols

Animals often symbolize human character types – a lion is usually bold; a peacock, proud; and so on. You can use them in stories to reinforce the type of character they are. Or you can make them behave the opposite to their stereotype: like the nervous Lion in *The Wizard of Oz* or Kenneth Grahame's gentle, friendly *Reluctant Dragon*.

Weather symbols

Weather that echoes a character's feelings can be used to create atmosphere. If your hero is unhappy, rain might reflect that sadness, just as sunshine could reflect a character's happiness and joy. Fog could reinforce a character's feelings of being lost or confused.

Select one of the titles below, or make up your own. Then choose some symbols to plan the story around.

- Red Snow
- The Lion Who Was Afraid
- Bottled Sunshine

Springboard

ACTIVITY

Use weather or animal symbols in a fantasy story, such as one about a talking animal or a superhero, or an underground world that nobody's discovered before. Try writing *The Country Where the Sun Never Shone.* Why doesn't it shine? Who arrives to change all that?

PACE AND TIMING

Stories are often about journeys: from place to place or through time. There are also emotional and personal journeys, as characters deal with events. **Pace** and timing are useful tools for inviting the reader to join the journey.

The journey starts

It's a good idea to work out roughly how many words your story will be before you start. Then you can decide how many words to use to set the scene and introduce the characters. If your story will be 1000 words long in total, the beginning will probably be no more than 200 words.

ACTIVITY

Write two different openings to a story with a maximum of 200 words each.

1. Introduce the main character, starting with their birth. Include something remarkable, such as being born in a strange place. By the end, the character is 12 years old and in the here-and-now.

2. The character is 12 years old already. It could be an ordinary day that becomes extraordinary, or a special day for them. Help the reader to find out as much as possible about the character in 200 words.

How do the things we learn about the character differ between the first and second version? Which is more detailed? Are there more of the character's thoughts and feelings in the second?

Setting the pace

Deciding how to divide up the text across the whole piece of writing is called pacing. It is no good writing lots of detail for the first three-quarters of your story and then having to hurry the story-telling at the end.

Speed up and slow down

Pace also refers to how you tell the story. Vary the pace of your story-telling to avoid sounding monotonous.

- Long sentences, with **subclauses** and commas, slow down the story-telling.
- Words with long vowel sounds – oa, ee, ai – also relax the pace.
- Short sentences or phrases speed up the pace and add excitement.

The long and short of it

Read these two paragraphs. Each contains just 42 words, but the first covers more than 60 years, the other, less than 60 seconds.

Over sixty years, I had crossed every continent. I allowed my gaze to wander the length and depth of the wide blue sky. Every vapour trail seemed to lead away from me, far away to the distant horizon, inviting me to follow.

Suddenly there was a bang on the roof. Crash! Right above my head. I gave a yelp. A flash of orange outside the window made me recoil. My throat tightened. I struggled to swallow. "It can't be!" I croaked. But it was.

Springboard

Write a story based on one of these journeys:

- Through the tunnel
- Over the rainbow
- Below the surface

Include at least one unusual form of transport – anything from a camel train to a parachute.

Tip

When you describe things, try to involve all five senses: touch, sight, sound, taste and smell.

Time phrases

A way of showing a passage of time is to use a time **phrase**. 'Shortly' and 'soon' mean much the same, but varying the phrases you use will spice up your writing. Here are some useful time phrases:

- soon
- shortly
- it was some time before
- before long
- meanwhile
- within the hour
- two weeks later
- after a while
- the following afternoon
- the next day
- until then
- over the next few days
- at first
- at last
- suddenly
- all at once
- just at that moment
- long ago
- as fast as
- for a second
- while
- during
- no sooner had... than...

BREAKING WRITER'S BLOCK

Have you ever woken up bursting with a desire to write and found your brain won't join in – you have no ideas of what to write about, your mind is a blank? All writers get this from time to time. It's known as writer's block. Here are some ideas to kick-start your story-writing…

Better late than never

A fool and his/her money are soon parted

Absence makes the heart grow fonder

Choose a **proverb** or saying and plan a story that proves its truth. Here are some to start you off…

Where there's a will there's a way

Never, never, never…

Parents and teachers tell us things that we MUST NOT do! Mindmap a never-never list, for example:

NEVER TELL ANYONE ABOUT THE TIGER

NEVER TOUCH THE RED BUTTON

NEVER GO THROUGH THE GREEN GATE

NEVER PICK UP A SPOTTED SNAIL

Choose one of the warnings and decide what happens when your main character ignores it!

Disaster!

In real life, stories often revolve around an accident or a mistake. Describe an accident that happened to you or that you caused. It can be as small as tripping over a shoelace or dropping a take-away meal, or as big as a car crash or falling off a swing. Add a little imagination and poetic licence (the author's 'right' to change things slightly). Can you develop it into a story?

Or try one of these titles*:

- A Broken Ankle
- Cat Catastrophe
- Mistaken Identity
- The Forgotten Letter
- Wrong Time; Wrong Place

* These are working titles – a title to call your story while you are writing it. It's often best to leave the final title until your story is complete. It should be one that intrigues people, making them want to read your story, but without giving too much away.

Tip

When developing an idea, try to think as widely as possible of ways of interpreting your seed of an idea so that it will grow beautifully. Use a spidergram to mindmap words and phrases.

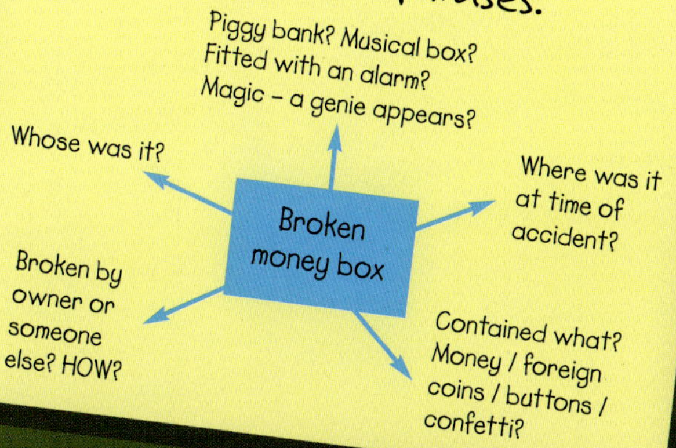

Springboard

Have a go at automatic writing. That is writing where you pick up your pen and write whatever comes into your head. You might even start by writing the same word over and over, until another pops into your head. The point is you ARE writing and – like an artist sketching before painting – a part of your automatic writing may grow into a story.

STORIES IN CHAPTERS

Short stories are fun to write – but how about a novel or **novella**? Here are some of the good things about writing a longer story.

You can...

- develop characters in greater depth, until they seem as real as your friends.
- take your characters through more experiences and to more locations.
- spend longer describing the setting and create different moods to complement the action.

One way to start...

If the idea of a novel is scary, try writing a series of short stories about one character, with a plot thread that links the stories. Join them as chapters in one book to create an **episodic** novel. Make sure that the plot is resolved in the final chapter.

For example, you might have a character who plays pranks on people. Each chapter – a story in its own right – tells of a trick he's played. At the same time, all those who have had tricks played on them, prepare to get their own back. They build up their friendship and plan revenge. The story reaches a climax as the joker is tricked in return.

ACTIVITY

Create a character with a problem – such as a girl who is struggling with homework. In trying to solve her problem, she creates a second one and so on. For example, her friend comes round and spills orange juice on both their books. In Chapter 3 they wipe their books, not knowing that the cloth has been used for bleach and they bleach the sofa... and so they go on until, in the final chapter, the problems are solved.

Tip

If you use a word-processing program to write on a computer it makes it easy to cut and paste text. It means you can add a chapter in the middle of the book, if you want, without any rewriting.

Chapter know-how

As you add more detail to any story, it will get longer and you can divide it into chapters. Make sure each chapter ends on a cliffhanger – a tantalizing line that makes the reader want to turn the page and read on. The start of each chapter must grab their attention, too, just as the first line of Chapter One did.

Springboard

Plan and write a story in five chapters, using the titles below. Don't forget the cliffhangers!

Chapter 1	A Step Too Far
Chapter 2	Waiting
Chapter 3	What a Find!
Chapter 4	Many Hands Make Light Work
Chapter 5	Just Rewards

ACTIVITY

Can you write a chapter that ends with one of these cliffhangers?

- When at last he woke, all he saw were stars in the purple sky above.
- There was only one thing for it: she would have to jump.
- Four more days of this!
- It was now or never. I took a deep breath and knocked on the door.

When you have finished, try to write the next chapter. Make sure the ending is a real page-turning cliffhanger.

Springboard

Now try a six-chapter book linking these chapter titles:

Chapter 1	The Pink Piano
Chapter 2	A Strange Teacher
Chapter 3	Making Excuses
Chapter 4	Music on Mars
Chapter 5	A Missing Note
Chapter 6	Home Again

JOINING THE DOTS

See how ingenious you can be at plotting a story that has to include certain, unconnected words at least once each.

These two story plans include each word from the list on the right. Both plans link the words into a storyline, but in a different order.

List of words
- dandelion
- camera
- flew
- pocket
- soup

(Note: It is fine to use the words more than once!)

Plan 1

Mum asks you to pick dandelion leaves for salad. Pick a few – gets boring. Start blowing dandelion clocks. Seeds flew over next-door's fence. Old lady next door angry – doesn't want weeds in her veg patch – marches round to your mum. Mum invites old lady to stay to lunch. Old lady (Maud) delighted – says looks too good to eat: pulls camera out of pocket & photographs it before enjoying eating. Next day she pops round with home-grown leeks & potatoes. Digs recipe for leek & potato soup out of her pocket. You decide to cook it for dinner. You take photograph of finished soup. Ending: You, mum & old lady neighbour share more recipes & produce Community Cook Book – raises money for old people's drop-in centre (as old lady has said how lonely she is).

Plan 2

Outdoor picnic. Something looking like dandelion seed flew into cup of soup. Starts to grow. Shock! Amazement! Grab camera to photo as it grows rapidly. See woman walking by – struggling with her coat as seed begun growing in pocket. Same everywhere. Seeds growing in unlikely places. Young plants sprout legs & jump out, running in one direction. Everyone follows, huge space-ship descends, green creatures enter it. Disappears in space. People left dumbfounded – except central character. He/she has one last seedling: a miniature alien to keep as a pet/secret friend called…Dandelion!

(Note: this one is briefer; details need adding)

Note how one story is realistic, the other fantasy; but both started with the same list of words.

ACTIVITY

Choose a set of words from below. Write the words on bits of paper and shuffle them in any order.

- Let one or two words suggest the beginning of a story – a setting, character or event.
- Make brief notes as ideas come to you, perhaps using a spidergraph.
- Develop your notes into a simple story plan. These are the 'dots' that you will join up as you write your story.

Now 'join the dots' by thinking up an attention-grabbing start to your story and then carry on writing to the end.

Tip

There's no need to use full sentences in your story plan!

Set 1. bone sneezed window suitcase onions

Set 2. drum valuable spoon swam magnet

Set 3. helicopter address butterfly sunset danced giraffe

Set 4. box bald mountain enormous circle purple

Set 5. arrow rainbow owl middle castle hungry safe

Set 6. trip lake dragon peaceful party tore twenty abandoned

Set 7. Saturday damaged lonely ice guitar growl danced chicken

Tip

If there is a word that seems tricky to fit in, use a spidergraph and see what ideas you come up with.

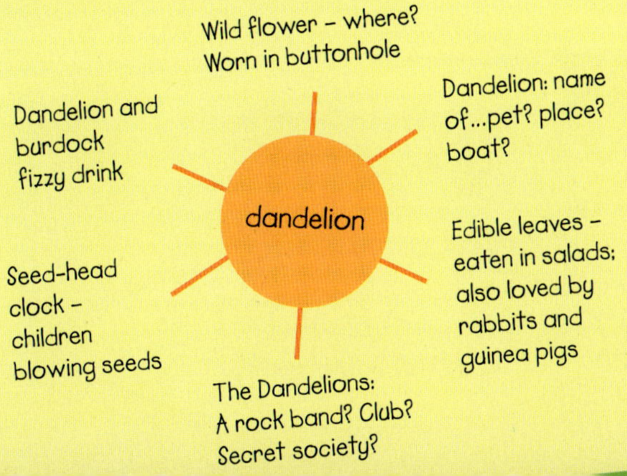

Springboard

- Think up more word lists to inspire 'join-the-dots' stories and swap them with your friends.
- Ask each family member to give you one word. Combine these into a list.
- Play a word-building game (such as Scrabble®) or complete a crossword. Then choose half a dozen words you have made for a word list.

STORY-MAPPING

Remember to decide early on from whose viewpoint you are telling the story.

Sometimes a writer's head can be buzzing with ideas. How do you decide which idea to develop from a number of different ones that all seem like good plot twists? Here's a way to sort out all your ideas and choose which ones to include and which to throw out. It's called a story-map.

A story-map makes it much easier to make sense of your ideas. Every time you make a decision your story changes direction. You end up writing a different story from what it would have been if you had made a different choice. Have a look at the story-map on the page opposite. A boy is setting off on holiday with his family. Where are they going and by what means of transport? Something unexpected is going to happen...

ACTIVITY

Follow the arrows from the top of the story-map opposite to choose a story-route. Write each choice on a sheet of paper. When you reach a question mark, use your imagination to make up the end of the story. When you have finished, you can draw up a storyboard (see page 15) to decide the order of events.

At this point, you can alter the order in which you describe events to the reader.

For example, you might begin your story with the boy knocking on a small cottage door. The cottage belongs to somebody whose phone number he rang earlier, when he found it in the glove compartment of the hire-car. (You can explain why the family hired a car later in the story.) It means that you can grab the reader's attention with an exciting part of the plot, drawing them into the story right from page one.

Springboard

Try finishing this story-map and see where it leads ...

THE HOLIDAY

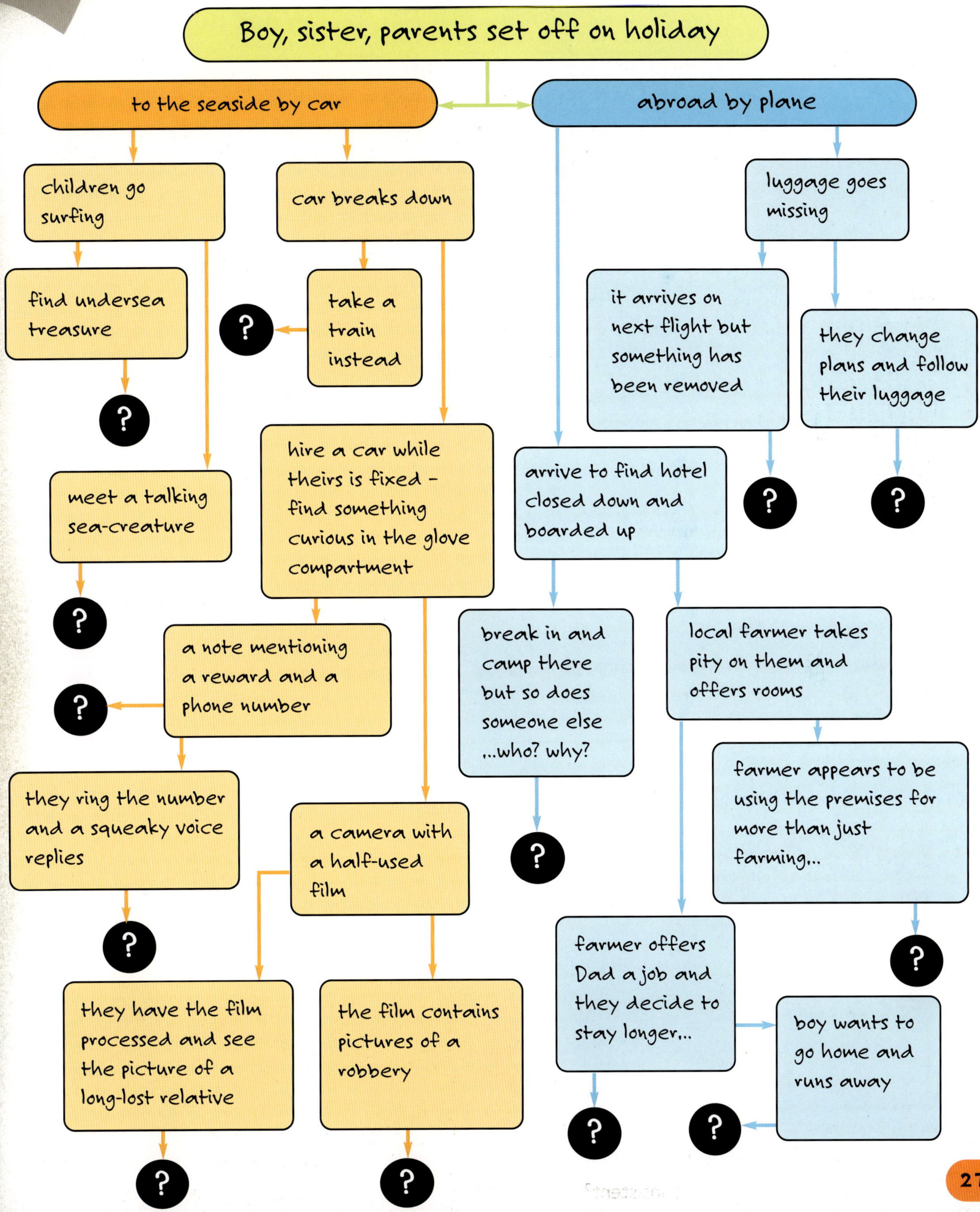
Boy, sister, parents set off on holiday
to the seaside by car
abroad by plane
children go surfing
car breaks down
luggage goes missing
find undersea treasure
take a train instead
it arrives on next flight but something has been removed
they change plans and follow their luggage
?
meet a talking sea-creature
hire a car while theirs is fixed – find something curious in the glove compartment
arrive to find hotel closed down and boarded up
a note mentioning a reward and a phone number
break in and camp there but so does someone else ...who? why?
local farmer takes pity on them and offers rooms
farmer appears to be using the premises for more than just farming...
they ring the number and a squeaky voice replies
a camera with a half-used film
farmer offers Dad a job and they decide to stay longer...
boy wants to go home and runs away
they have the film processed and see the picture of a long-lost relative
the film contains pictures of a robbery

SUMMING UP

Planning characters, setting, plot, opening lines, viewpoint… what a lot of things an author has to weave together to create a story! The main thing – if you enjoy writing – is to stick at it. Keep practising. Here are some reminders.

Reminder checklist

Here are some things to remember when writing stories.

- Make sure first lines grab attention.
- Show rather than tell.
- Experiment with different voices – write in different characters.
- Use dialogue to break up narrative.
- Read aloud and rewrite to improve the flow.
- Use all five senses in description.
- Vary your sentence length to change pace.
- Tie up any loose ends before the close of your story.
- Create a happy ending – satisfying for the reader.
- End chapters with a page-turning cliff-hanger.
- Check and 'proof-read' your story:
  - Do all pronouns agree with their subjects?
  - Is your continuity of action accurate?
  - Have you overused certain words?
  - Have you checked spellings?
  - Is your use of tense consistent?

What next?

Now that your writing is finished, here are some things to do with it:

- Start a writers' club with like-minded friends. Read your stories to each other. Give and take helpful critiques (constructive critical comments on your writing). No author ever stops learning how to improve!
- Produce a short-story **anthology** with your friends, containing a story by each of you.
- Desk-top publish your stories – adding illustrations – on your computer. You could staple them together to create a whole library of your own books!

- Get together with friends to publish a magazine for other friends and family to enjoy.

- Look out for writing competitions to enter. These are often advertised in libraries and bookshops. Some appear on websites – but check who is running them first. Are they a well-established publisher or arts group? Do they have a junior section? Are they free to enter? Check with an adult first.

Springboard 1

Try developing any of these ideas as stories:

Something appears... in the steam of the kettle... through the window... in the mirror... on the computer... or a presenter speaks to you from the TV screen... WHAT HAPPENS NEXT?

Springboard 2

A child goes to the aid of an old person who has fallen down. What happens next? Maybe the two find that they have something unlikely in common, such as odd socks or very elderly pet goldfish. Perhaps the old person gives their helper a reward - where does that lead them next?

Springboard 3

You find a ball which, when it bounces, does something magical – it always goes where you kick or throw it; it glows and hums and an alien emerges; or it bursts like a balloon and suddenly snow falls in summer? Think of a reason to explain the magical event. For example, snow might help penguins that are overheating in the local zoo.

GLOSSARY

Anthology collection of stories by different authors

Author person who creates and writes a book

Chapter a division of text within a longer narrative; one section of a book

Character a fictional person in a book

Copyright the author's right of ownership of an original text

Dialogue direct speech between characters

Direct speech writing words as spoken ("I love you," he said.)

Edit to alter or rewrite, often removing or replacing words

Episodic written in episodes (parts) which describe a series of events

Fable a legendary story not based on fact, often with a moral or a message

Facts things that are true rather than imaginary or made up

Fantasy imaginary creation which could never be real

Fiction created from the imagination; not true or factual

Genre type of writing with a specific style and purpose

Legend a traditional historical story sometimes believed to be fact but without factual evidence

Mindmap to think of anything and everything related to one subject

Narrative another word for story

Novel an extended story, usually divided into chapters

Novella a short novel

Pace the speed at which the action happens

Paragraph a division within longer text which contains several sentences on a similar theme or subject matter

Phrase a group of words

Plot plan of a sequence of connected events with an outcome developed from the start

Protagonist central character or hero to whom the reader can relate

Proverb a saying with a moral to it that offers advice through sharing human experience

Sentence a series of words that make sense and include a verb (a doing- or action-word)

Storyboard to plan a story using a picture sequence of the main scenes

Subclause a phrase within a sentence, separated by commas each side

Symbol something that becomes a sign, representing an idea or meaning beyond itself

Tense the form a verb takes to indicate past, present or future (such as was, is, will be)

Text the words on the page

INDEX

PARENT AND TEACHER NOTES

- Small children are natural story tellers. Watch them in a playground planning the characters, scenario and events of a game of mothers and fathers, cops and robbers, goodies and baddies – they are never short of ideas. As they get older, many children will happily develop this inventive talent into the written word. Others may need encouragement. This book aims to kick-start the writing habit and help children, not just to make a start, but stick at it and see their story ideas grow from a seed of an idea to fruition. Nothing succeeds like success.

- This book aims to encourage and improve the art of story-telling. It gives ideas and advice. Its main purpose is to persuade children to 'let go' and really develop their art. At first, this may be at the expense of niceties such as spelling. Do not worry too much about this. The main thing is that the child is getting his or her ideas down on paper. There is plenty of time later to correct spellings, punctuation and so forth. In fact, proof-reading and rewriting are discussed in the book.

- You can help your children's efforts in lots of ways. Always be willing to read their stories – but only when they invite you to do so. Never pressure them into telling you beforehand what they are writing about or how the story will end. They may not know until after they've written it!

- When you do read their story they will be dying to know what you think of it. Mainly – did you enjoy it? Always find something positive to say that will encourage your child to continue writing. Anyone, young or old, will automatically improve at an art the more they practise it. They can discover for themselves how much progress they've made as time goes by. Encourage them to keep examples of their early efforts so that they will be able to observe their improvement.

- Be prepared to offer help in their writing if they ask for it. They may come up against frustrating plotting anomalies that hadn't occurred to them and are spoiling the completion of their story. (A penguin is crucial to the plot and the setting is a desert!) It may be that, through discussion, they can find a way around their problem. (Make it a vulture instead of a penguin or move the setting to the Antarctic!)

- Please try not to laugh at your child's early efforts – even if they are side-splittingly funny when they're not meant to be. Feelings are easily hurt.

- Often struggling readers and children with literacy difficulties can nonetheless have very creative minds. If your child is bursting with ideas for stories but struggles to get them down on paper, offer to be their secretary, writing to their dictation. Alternatively, encourage them to use a voice recorder and help them to transcribe their story later.